LOVEYS

"Rat"

"PreTTY"

"Deeba"

GARY PREISER MD, FAAP

To order additional copies of this book, contact:
Xlibris
1-888-795-4274
www.Xlibris.com
Orders@Xlibris.com

ISBN: 978-1-9845-7912-6 (sc)
ISBN: 978-1-9845-7913-3 (hc)
ISBN: 978-1-9845-7948-5 (e)

Library of Congress Control Number: 2020908836

Print information available on the last page

Rev. date: 05/14/2020

LOVEYS

"PreTTY"   "RaT"   "Deeba"

By Gary Preiser MD, FAAP
Retired Pediatrician

Dedication

To our daughter Sarah
June 13, 1978–December 28, 2001

Acknowledgement

To my sister, Cheryl Leopold, for her tireless editing and energizing of this book, Richard Leopold for his technical advice, and my dear wife Lynda for her patience and support.

CONTENTS

Introduction

When you were a little baby, everyone in your family wanted to touch and hold you because they loved you so much. Your mom, your dad, your grandmas and grandpas, your aunts and uncles and your brothers and sisters, if you have any, all wanted a turn holding and hugging you. They all wanted to give you something to hold and hug, a Lovey that they could get from Lovey Land. This Lovey might be a special blanket, a doll or a very cute stuffed animal such as a bear, a lamb, a chipmunk, a cow or any other animal on a farm or in a zoo. You might like all these presents but will probably pick one to be special, to sleep with, to carry around and to cuddle with. That will be your special Lovey and when you can say words, you can give your Lovey a name such as: Blankie, Buh-Buh, Horsey, Woof-Woof, or Freedie or Mugga or your own special word. You might surprise everyone and just pick a cloth diaper as your Lovey and give it a name. What do you call your Lovey?

Anyway, your Lovey might go everywhere with you: on car rides, to your crib or bed to help you sleep every night, to doctor visits to help you be brave. You might be unhappy if you forget your Lovey so don't lose it. Loveys sometimes get torn, or lose an eye or an ear so someone in your family will have to repair it. That's no problem, and as it gets more and more worn, it gets more and more special. There is no rule for giving up a Lovey, but eventually they seem to find their way into trunks and closets often to be found in later years sparking fond memories.

So, enjoy your Lovey and enjoy the photographs of the children with their Loveys and reading these little stories about how they got their Loveys and the things they do. Every word is true!

Maybe you can draw a picture and write a story about your Lovey too!

Grandma gave me to Dameon. I, "MooMoo" the cow, actually replaced "Mine," Dameon's blanket, and now I am the first request at bedtime and go everywhere with him.

I am "Binky," the blanket, and have been with Danni since she was an infant. I get rubbed so much that I often need to be repaired. I go to the store and for car rides with Danni, but I like it best bunched up under her cheek when she sleeps. If she forgets me when she goes for a car ride, Dad has to turn the car around to get me or Danni is very sad.

Even though I've only been with Crystal for 2 months, I go to all her doctor appointments. I'm "Cheyenne," an Appaloosa horse, and I think my name is the best!

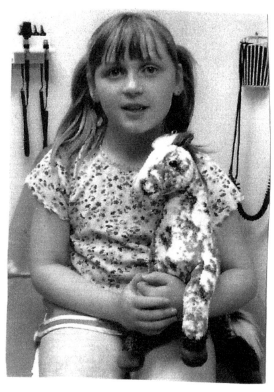

Matt calls me "Pretty," and we have been partners since he was 10 months old. I sleep with him and travel in the car, and I'm glad that he hugs me when he is upset. Dad was smart to buy several blankets in case one of me gets lost.

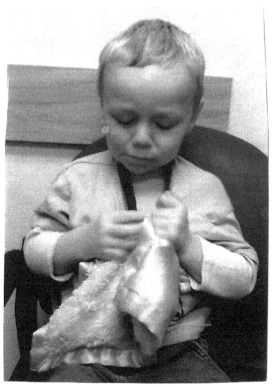

I was a present for Michael on his first birthday when he named me "Deeba." I get around a lot and have been to school for show-and-tell and stuffed animal day. Dad embroidered a new nose and mouth on me, and Michael added the red collar and bells. Mom says they don't make "Deebas" like me anymore.

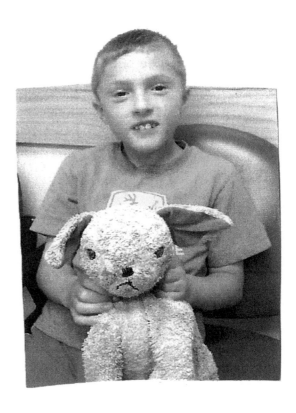

"Night-Night" is a funny name but that's what Alexis calls me. Actually I'm number four of the 10 Lovey blankets that Mom bought. Three have already been lost in various stores. Alexis comforts herself by rubbing my silky binding along her nose, and I think she likes the way I smell since she whines when I'm washed. She also whines a lot if they forget to take me on a trip.

"Night Night"

Call me "Vuh Vuh." I guess I look like a pacifier to you. Luke likes to keep me in his mouth especially when he goes to sleep. Mom wants him to give me up for his third birthday so his teeth come in straight. He also has a blanket critter called "Buh Buh" who helps him fall asleep and relax on long car trips. "Buh Buh" has a silky label that Luke likes to rub against his face for comfort.

I'm "Woobie," a blanket with one soft flannel side and one shiny satin side. I go to sleep and everywhere with Ryan who sucks his right thumb while clutching me in the same hand. If you think that's tricky, he also makes a little tunnel where he can rub the fingers of his left hand at the same time. I feel very loved.

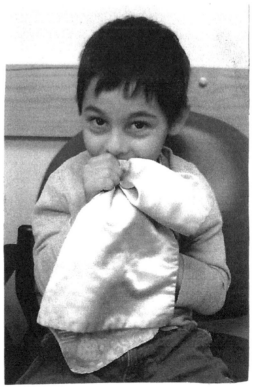

I'm "Lammy" the lamb, and, of course, I follow Samantha to school sometimes since I'm "Lammy" the lamb. I have been her always-friend for 5 years. I like to sleep with Samantha, but sometimes I need a repair by Grandma and miss a night.

I think my name is the best of all the Loveys because Gavin named me. I'm "Teddy-Orsa," and even though I've been with Gavin since birth, I've never needed any repairs. Maybe that's because he doesn't take me to school but keeps me for sleep and scary times like shots at the doctor's office.

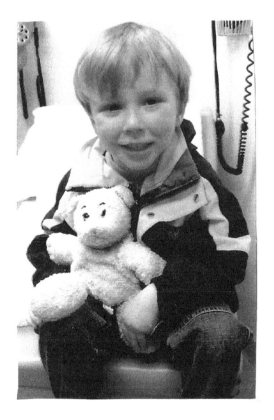

Mom and Dad both gave me to Keagan when he was born. I have the shortest name, "B," and I go everywhere with Keagan. He really likes to play with my label. Mom can only wash me when Keagan is asleep so he won't cry.

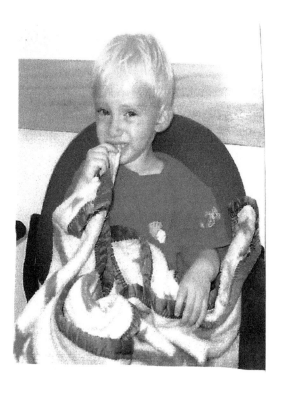

I'm "Pinky" the rabbit. I met Riannon when she was a baby and have been her friend ever since. Now she is 7 years old, and I do not go to school with her anymore, but I still ride with her in the car and go to doctor visits. Riannon's Grandma has patched me several times and even re-stuffed my neck. The fur is worn off my chest from a lot of loving.

My name is now "Pitty," but I started out as "Spitty," the burp cloth. I'm really just an old-fashioned cloth diaper. However, I have a slightly raised seam that Tanner likes to hold and rub with his fingers for comfort.

"Pitty"

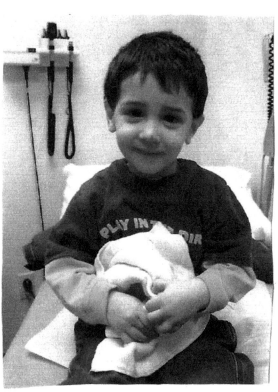

I am "Gookie," a bunny who was bought by Dad when Amy was 1 year old. I was afraid when I was left outside under a tree for two weeks, but they found me. I sleep with Amy, go to school, doctor visits and traveling. My ears have been sewn back on once, and my nose, which is missing now, was replaced twice. I hope I get a new nose soon.

I have been with Grace since she was 5 months old, and she thinks she will not accept any other "Bebe." However, our wise Mom has 5 "Bebes" that I know are at key places like Grandma's house and the babysitter's house. Grace cries and cries if they forget me, but as soon as she gets home, I get hugged and the tears turn to laughter.

"Bebe"

Abigail is very flexible with her Loveys as long as she has one to hug. I was the first "Elephant" by name. I was with her constantly until I was lost for a while when Abigail was 18 months old. It did not hurt my feelings when she found comfort with "Buffa," the black bear, then "Piggy" and now "Bubba," the blanket, who goes to day care with her because I'm back in the group. Such is the life of a Lovey.

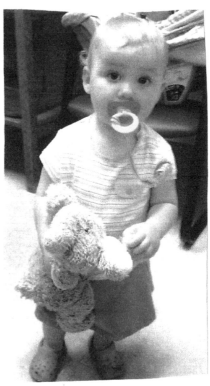

I am "Margaret" and was a Christmas present for Elena. I am a day toy, not for sleep. Elena nurses me and puts me to bed in a cradle. I think I'm a real baby. I also think Elena is a little camera shy!

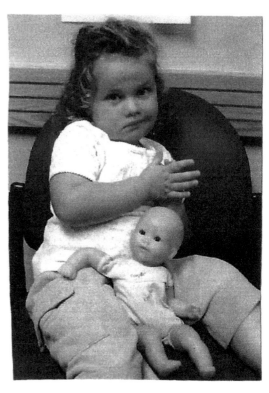

I may look just like "a knot in a diaper," but Ava has been very attached to me since she was 4 months old. She holds me in the hand that has the thumb in her mouth. It is easy to trick Ava, because Mom can switch to any of the 10 other diapers she has when I need to be washed. That way I'm always clean.

"a knot in a diaper"

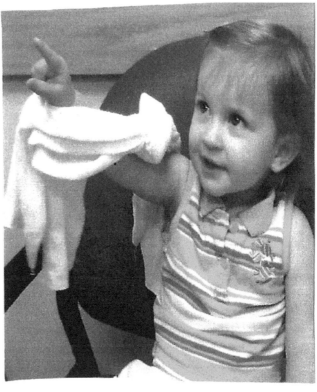

I'm "Cookie," the bear. Jodean's aunt gave her "Binny," the blanket, when she was born, and I joined them a little later. Now we are all best friends and go everywhere together and are NEVER forgotten.

Aliyah was born very small but is healthy now. She carries me with her during the day and tosses me on the floor to lie upon, but it doesn't hurt because I'm a blanket. I like when she rubs me against her face to help her go to sleep. I have no special name.

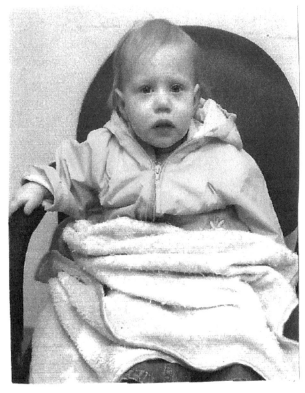

It's a little crowded on Natasha's lap with her two blankets, but I'm "Rat," and I don't even care when she takes the blankets to school or rolls one corner to a point to rub along her nose to fall asleep. That's because I'm her only Lovey with a name.

"Rat"

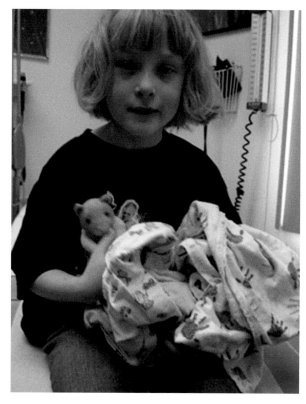

Draw a picture of your Lovey and tell its story

Matching Game

Put the number of the Lovey's name under its picture.

1. Pinky   2. Pitty   3. Cookie   4. Deeba   5. VuhVuh   6. "B"   7. Margaret
8. Binky   9. MooMoo   10. Pretty   11. Night-Night   12. Woobie   13. Lammy
14. Teddy-Orsa   15. Cheyenne   16. Rat   17. Gookie   18. BeBe   19. Elephant
20. Knot   22. no name ?

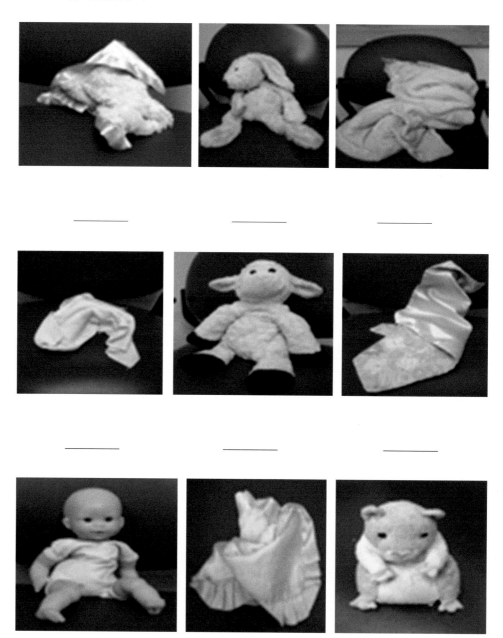

Matching Game

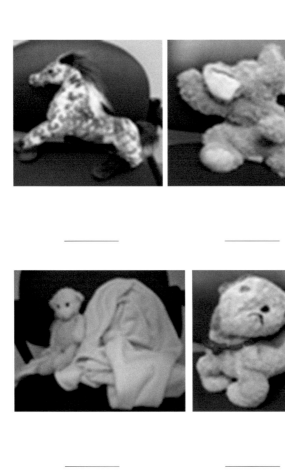
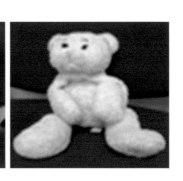

_____   _____   _____

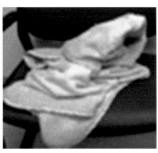

_____   _____   _____

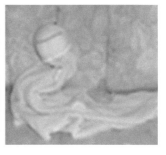

_____   _____   _____

Printed in the United States
By Bookmasters